"Booie" Paterson Chappell

Dean Wroth

All 'Bout Charleston

All 'Bout Charleston

text by *Ruth Paterson Chappell*
illustrations by *Dean Wroth*

SANDLAPPER PUBLISHING CO., INC.
ORANGEBURG, SOUTH CAROLINA

FIRST EDITION

Published by Sandlapper Publishing Co., Inc.
       Orangeburg, South Carolina

Printed in Korea

Library of Congress Cataloging-in-Publication Data

Chappell, Ruth Paterson.
    All 'bout Charleston / text by Ruth Paterson Chappell ;
illustrations by Dean Wroth. — 1st ed.
          p.   cm.
    Summary: Rhyming text for each letter of the alphabet explores the
city of Charleston, South Carolina, its history, and notable
features.
    ISBN 0-87844-144-1
    1. Charleston (S.C.)—Juvenile literature. 2. English language—
Alphabet—Juvenile literature. [1. Charleston (S.C.)
2. Alphabet.]   I. Wroth, Dean, ill.   II. Title.
F279.C44C47   1998
428.1—dc21
    [E]   97-51146
                                                        CIP
                                                         AC

Dedicated to

Adventurous, Book-loving Children

~Booie Chappell

my darling girls,
Sarah and Mary Kate

~Dean Wroth

All 'Bout Charleston

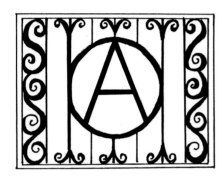

. . . is for ALPHABET.
This book will show
A new way to learn it
With places to go.

. . . *is for* BATTERY.

Have you been there today?

Let's find it together.

It's a great place to play.

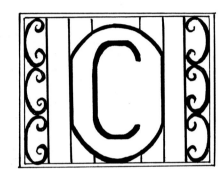

. . . is for CHURCH.

Charleston has quite a few
So it's called "Holy City."
I like that. Don't you?

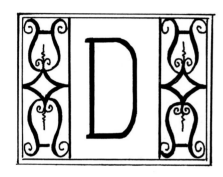

. . . *is for* DRAYTON,

The name of a house.

But it's called Drayton Hall.

Look for the mouse!

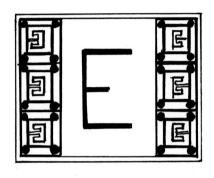

. . . is for ENGLAND,

The start of the trip

Made by settlers to Charleston

In a big sailing ship.

. . . is for FOUNTAIN—
Jump in when it's hot—
At Waterfront Park.
You'll like it a lot.

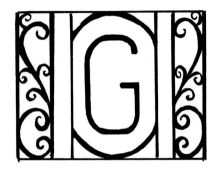

. . . is for GIBBES,

A museum of art

With programs for children.

When do we start?

. . . is for HARBOR

Where the water is wide

And sea gulls fly over

While baby crabs hide.

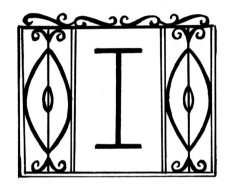

. . . is for ISLAND,

Land that looks like it floats.

It's surrounded by water.

People get there in boats.

. . . *is for* JAMES

And John is another.

They're both names for islands.

Are they names for your brothers?

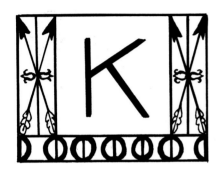

. . . is for KIAWAH,

An island as well.

It's an Indian word.

Did you guess? Could you tell?

. . . is for LANDING,

The place where they came

To build a new city.

Charles Towne is its name.

. . . is for MIDDLETON.

See Magnolia too.

Your family will love them.

And don't miss the zoo!

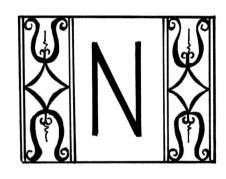

. . . is for NAVY.

The base that was here.

Now other big boats

Tie up to the pier.

. . . is for OCEAN

At the end of the land.

On the edge is the beach.

It's covered with sand.

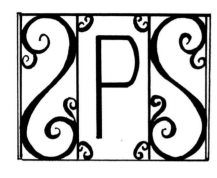

. . . *is for* PARK.

If I had to choose one,

I just couldn't do it.

They all are such fun.

. . . *is for* QUEEN,

The name of a street.

It crosses another

Where royalty meet.

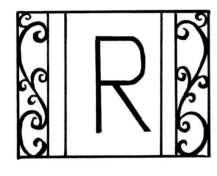

. . . is for RIVERS.

They flow with the tide

Going up and then down

Like a carnival ride.

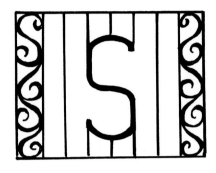

. . . is for SUMTER,
A fort you can see
Way out in the harbor.
You <u>could</u> climb a tree.

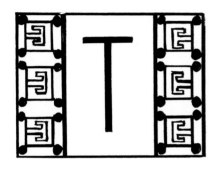

T. . . is for TRADD,
A street that was . . . maybe
Named after Robert,
Charleston's first little baby.

. . . *is for* UNDER,

A place that you'll know—
The Old Exchange Building.
To the dungeon you go!

. . . is for VISITORS,

The Center in town.

Go there for a map

That will show you around.

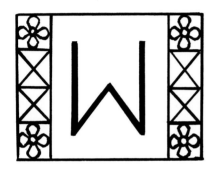

. . . is for WILDLIFE.

In our woods we still have it.

Walk softly, on tiptoe.

You might see a rabbit.

. . . is for TEN

On St. Michael's Church tower.

I'll bet you can find

Where it tells you the hour.

. . . is for YORKTOWN,

A historic ship.

Salute proudly while boarding

This floating airstrip.

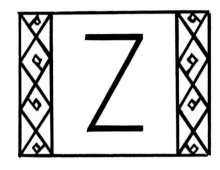

. . . is for Z-Z-Zs,

The sound when you snore.

Did you learn all your letters?

Say "Good night." Close the door!

~About the Author and Illustrator~

Ruth ("Booie") Paterson Chappell is on the education staff at Drayton Hall Plantation in Charleston, South Carolina. Booie received her BA in early childhood education from the University of Maryland and continued her graduate work at Towson State. Prior to moving to Charleston, she taught elementary school. She is a member of the Charleston Alumnae Association of Kappa Kappa Gamma, the South Carolina Historical Society, the Preservation Society of Charleston, and the National Trust for Historic Preservation. Booie and her husband, Chris, live on Drayton Hall Plantation, where they enjoy the entertaining antics of their young black Labrador retriever, Missy, and the frequent visits of their children and grandchildren.

Dean Gray Wroth is a free-lance artist. She received a BA in fine art from Marietta College in Ohio and is an active member of her local fine arts league. She previously served as arts and crafts supervisor with Maryland's Montgomery County Department of Recreation. Her interests include gardening, cooking, classical music, and ballet. Dean lives in Poolesville, Maryland, with her husband Ted and daughters Sarah and Mary Kate. They share their home with a terrific cat named Lizzy.

♥ Booie and Dean worked together previously on *The Mysterious Tail of a Charleston Cat* (© 1995), coauthored by Bess Paterson Shipe.

photo by Gene Heizer

. . . . A Book Contest

Please turn the page.

Now, are you ready?
Take a long careful look
And find, if you can,
All these things in this book. ⟶

It's not very hard,
And I'm sure that you'll try.
If you can't find them all,
PLEASE ... DON'T ... CRY!

A	anchor	N	numbers
B	bluebird	O	orange cat
C	crown	P	pirate hat
D	dog	Q	quills
E	easel	R	rooster
F	fish	S	sand dollar
G	glass	T	teddy bears
H	helicopter	U	umbrella
I	Indian	V	village
J	jeans	W	wagon
K	kitty	X	Xs
L	lamp	Y	yellow shoes
M	moon	Z	zero

That's *All 'Bout Charleston.*

THE DESIGN WORK, WHICH FRAMES EACH LETTER OF THE ALPHABET,
IS AN ADAPTATION OF AUTHENTIC CHARLESTON IRONWORK.